CAMBRIDGE PRIMARY
Science

Challenge

Jon Board and Alan Cross

CAMBRIDGE
UNIVERSITY PRESS

CAMBRIDGE
UNIVERSITY PRESS

University Printing House, Cambridge CB2 8BS, United Kingdom

One Liberty Plaza, 20th Floor, New York, NY 10006, USA

477 Williamstown Road, Port Melbourne, VIC 3207, Australia

314–321, 3rd Floor, Plot 3, Splendor Forum, Jasola District Centre, New Delhi – 110025, India

79 Anson Road, #06–04/06, Singapore 079906

Cambridge University Press is part of the University of Cambridge.

It furthers the University's mission by disseminating knowledge in the pursuit of education, learning and research at the highest international levels of excellence.

www.cambridge.org
Information on this title: www.cambridge.org/9781316611142

First published 2016

20 19 18 17 16 15 14 13 12 11 10

Produced for Cambridge University Press by
White-Thomson Publishing
www.wtpub.co.uk

Editor: Rachel Minay
Designer: Tracey Camden

Printed in Malaysia by Vivar Printing

A catalogue record for this publication is available from the British Library

ISBN 978-1-316-61114-2 Paperback

....

Contents

Introduction

This series of primary science activity books complements *Cambridge Primary Science* and progresses, through practice, learner confidence and depth of knowledge in the skills of scientific enquiry (SE) and key scientific vocabulary and concepts. These activity books will:

- enhance and extend learners' scientific knowledge and facts
- promote scientific enquiry skills and learning in order to think like a scientist
- advance each learner's knowledge and use of scientific vocabulary and concepts in their correct context.

The *Challenge* activity books extend learners' understanding of the main curriculum, providing an opportunity to increase the depth of their knowledge and scientific enquiry skills from a key selection of topics. This workbook does not cover all of the curriculum framework content for this stage.

How to use the activity books

These activity books have been designed for use by individual learners, either in the classroom or at home. As teachers and as parents, you can decide how and when they are used by your learner to best improve their progress. The *Challenge* activity books target specific topics (lessons) from Grades 1–6 from all the units covered in *Cambridge Primary Science*. This targeted approach has been carefully designed to consolidate topics where help is most needed.

How to use the units

Unit introduction

Each unit starts with an introduction for you as the teacher or parent. It clearly sets out which topics are covered in the unit and the learning objectives of the activities in each section. This is where you can work with learners to select all, most or just one of the sections according to individual needs.

The introduction also provides advice and tips on how best to support the learner in the skills of scientific enquiry and in the practice of key scientific vocabulary.

At this grade, it is very likely the learners are still learning to read, so teacher/parent may need to explain these verbally.

Sections

Each section matches a corresponding lesson in the main series. Sections contain write-in activities that are supported by:

- Key words – key vocabulary for the topic, also highlighted in bold in the sections
- Key facts – a short fact to support the activities where relevant
- Look and learn – where needed, activities are supported with scientific exemplars for extra support of how to treat a concept or scientific method
- Remember – tips for the learner to steer them in the right direction.

How to approach the write-in activities

Teachers and parents are advised to provide students with a blank A5 notebook at the start of each grade for learners to use alongside these activity books. Most activities will provide enough space for the answers required. However, some learner responses – especially to enquiry-type questions – may require more space for notes. Keeping notes and plans models how scientists work and encourages learners to explore and record their thinking, leaving the activity books for the final, more focused answers.

Think about it questions

Each unit also contains some questions for discussion at home with parents, or at school. Although learners will record the outcomes of their discussions in the activity book, these questions are intended to encourage the students to think more deeply.

Self-assessment

Each section in the unit ends with a self-assessment opportunity for learners: empty circles with short learning statements. Teachers or parents can ask learners to complete the circles in a number of ways, depending on their age and preference, e.g. with faces, traffic light colours or numbers. The completed self-assessments provide teachers with a clearer understanding of how best to progress and support individual learners.

Glossary of key words and concepts

At the end of each activity book there is a glossary of key scientific words and concepts arranged by unit. Learners are regularly reminded to practise saying these words out loud and in sentences to improve communication skills in scientific literacy.

1 Going outside

The unit challenge

The activities in this Challenge unit will extend learners' knowledge of the following topics in the Learner's Book and Activity Book:

Topic	In this topic, learners will:
1.1 Different places to live	make predictions then check them by investigation
1.2 Can we care for our environment?	consider why we should look after the environment
1.3 Our weather	see Skills Builder, Section 1.3
1.4 Extreme weather	practise taking measurements

Help your learner

In this unit, learners will practise making predictions (Section 1.1), identifying simple patterns in evidence (Section 1.2) and taking measurements (Section 1.4). To help them:

1 In Section 1.1, encourage learners to develop observational skills and an interest in wildlife by asking them to be responsible for a small outdoor area. This could be a small flowerbed or even a tiny garden made in a large flowerpot or window box. Small ponds can be created using plastic containers and a little soil, but the water level would need to be topped up often in hot climates.

2 For Section 1.4, learners could make regular observations and measurements of normal and extreme weather. They could also record the day's temperature and rainfall.

! Learners will need adult help for Section 1.1.

TEACHING TIP

Help learners to explore and look after the environment. Talk with them about litter, pollution and climate change and possible solutions to these problems.

1.1 Different places to live

different, environment, predict

Comparing environments

Choose two **different environments** where you can look for animals.

1 **Predict** whether the environments will have many animals or only a few.

Environment	
	many animals ☐
	few animals ☐
	many animals ☐
	few animals ☐

2 Count the animals you find in each environment.

Environment	Number of animals

> ⚠️ Look out for plants that sting and animals that bite. Ask an adult to help you.

3 Which environment has more animals? _____

4 Draw an animal you find.

5 Think about it!

Were your predictions correct? _____

CHECK YOUR LEARNING

○ I can compare different environments.

○ I can make predictions and find out if they are right.

paper,
forest,
protect

LOOK AND LEARN

Paper is made from wood.

Looking after forests

This **forest** is being cut down to make paper.

Scientists are counting the animals that live in the forest.

This is what they find out.

Month	Jan	Feb	Mar	Apr	May	Jun
Number of animals	55	54	50	42	33	25

1 What has happened to the number of animals? Tick one box.

gone up ☐

gone down ☐

stayed the same ☐

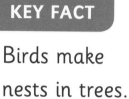

2 Why might there be fewer birds living in the forest in June?

_____

_____

3 **Think about it!**

We need paper, but in what ways can we **protect** the animals?

_____

_____

CHECK YOUR LEARNING

◯ I know about ways to protect the environment.

measure, temperature, thermometer, rain gauge, extreme

Measuring the weather

Julia and Bo are **measuring** the weather.

1 Measure the **temperature** on each **thermometer**.

Monday	Tuesday	Wednesday
°C 45 40 35 30 25 20 15 10 5 0 -5	°C 45 40 35 30 25 20 15 10 5 0 -5	°C 45 40 35 30 25 20 15 10 5 0 -5
_____ °C	_____ °C	_____ °C

2 Which day was extremely hot? _____

3 Measure the rain in the **rain gauge**.

Monday	Tuesday	Wednesday
cl 40 35 30 25 20 15 10 5 0	cl 40 35 30 25 20 15 10 5 0	cl 40 35 30 25 20 15 10 5 0
_____ cl	_____ cl	_____ cl

4 Which day had **extreme** rain? _____

5 Think about it!

What can you do to look after yourself in extreme hot weather?
Tick or cross each box.

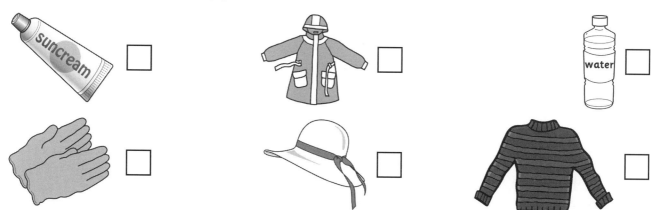

CHECK YOUR LEARNING

◯ I can measure carefully.

◯ I can compare weather data.

2 Looking at rocks

The unit challenge

The activities in this Challenge unit will extend learners' knowledge of the following topics from the Learner's Book and Activity Book:

Topic	In this topic, learners will:
2.1 What are rocks?	see Skills Builder, Section 2.1
2.2 Uses of rocks	decide on the best material for a roof based on the results of an investigation
2.3 Soil	investigate how much water different soils absorb
2.4 Other natural materials	see Skills Builder, Section 2.4

Help your learner

In this unit, learners will practise making observations to answer a science question (Sections 2.2 and 2.3), using first-hand experience and making comparisons (Sections 2.2 and 2.3). They will also identify when tests are unfair (Sections 2.2 and 2.3). To help them:

TEACHING TIP

Many learners will enjoy learning the names of types of rocks, such as granite, basalt, shale, flint, marble and limestone.

1 In Section 2.2, help learners to test whether rocks hold water. Put three small drops of water on the surface of each rock and watch whether it is absorbed. Check whether the water has been absorbed or has simply spread out by touching the surface of the rock with a paper towel. The wetter the towel, the less water was absorbed by the rock.

2 In Section 2.3, allow learners to squeeze sponges in water. Show them the holes in the sponge and ask them to explain why the sponge can absorb water. Can they explain where the bubbles come from? Explain to learners that soil is a bit like a sponge. It has small holes full of air that can absorb water.

waterproof, chalk, slate, sandstone

Which rock makes a good roof?

Mia is helping her Dad build a house.

She is testing the rocks to see if they are **waterproof**.

1 Which rock has soaked up all of the water?

_____

2 Which rock has soaked up some of the water?

_____

3 Which rock is waterproof?

_____

4 Which rock would make a good roof?

_____

5 Think about it!

What can Mia keep the same to make her test fair?

_____

CHECK YOUR LEARNING

◯ I can use a science test to answer questions.

◯ I know that some rocks are waterproof.

Water in soil

You will need a plant pot with holes at the bottom, a bottle of water, a large measuring jug, a timer and two different kinds of **soil**.

Look at the picture to see what to do.

You are going to measure how many centilitres of water come through the soil.

1 **What will you do to make the test fair? Tick two boxes.**

Use the same amount of water for each soil. ☐

Use a different amount of water for each soil. ☐

Measure the water when you like. ☐

Measure the water after two minutes both times. ☐

2 Write your results in the table.

	Soil A	Soil B
How many centilitres of water after two minutes?	_____ cl	_____ cl

3 Which soil let more water through? _____

KEY FACT

Plants get water from the soil.

water

4 Which soil can hold more water for the plants? _____

5 **Think about it!**

Is water a natural or man-made material?

_____

CHECK YOUR LEARNING

◯ I can use a fair test to compare soils.

3 Changing materials

The unit challenge

The activities in this Challenge unit will extend learners' knowledge of the following topics from the Learner's Book and Activity Book:

Topic	In this topic, learners will:
3.1 Materials changing shape	investigate ways to change the shape of materials and record observations in a table
3.2 Bending and twisting	see Skills Builder, Section 3.2
3.3 Fantastic elastic	see Skills Builder, Section 3.3
3.4 Heating and cooling	see Skills Builder, Section 3.4
3.5 Why is the sea salty?	try to dissolve different solids in water and use first-hand evidence

Help your learner

In this unit, learners will use first-hand experience and make and record observations (Sections 3.1 and 3.5). They will also practise explaining what happened (Sections 3.1 and 3.5). To help them:

1 Help learners to remember the vocabulary in Section 3.1 by making up actions to go with each word. Learners could play a moving game such as 'Simon Says' to practise using the words and the actions.

2 When dissolving sugar in Section 3.5, learners could be encouraged to explore the effect of the temperature of the water. The warmer water is, the more sugar will dissolve in it.

TEACHING TIP

Explain that 'elastic', 'flexible' and 'rigid' are words that tell us what a material is like. These are called properties of materials. Learners will learn more about properties of materials in Stage 3.

LOOK AND LEARN

Materials that can **bend**, **squash**, **stretch** or **twist** are called **flexible** materials.

Materials that cannot bend, squash, stretch or twist are called **rigid** materials.

Materials that will stretch and then go back into shape are called **elastic** materials.

Changing materials

You will need a sheet of paper, a metal paper clip, a rubber band, a metal coin and a plastic ruler.

1 Try to bend, squash, stretch and twist each object.

2 Fill in the table. One has been started for you.

Object	Material	Bend	Squash	Stretch	Twist	Is it rigid or flexible?	Is it elastic?
sheet of paper	paper	✓	✓	✗	✓	flexible	no
paper clip							
rubber band							
coin							
ruler							

3 Think about it!

The paper clip and the coin are both metal, but one is flexible and the other is rigid. Why are they different?

_____

_____

CHECK YOUR LEARNING

◯ I can record my observations in a table.

◯ I can compare ways that different materials can be changed.

3.5 Why is the sea salty?

dissolve

Dissolving different solids

You will need flour, sand, sugar, a sweet, a spoon and warm water.

1 Try **dissolving** these solids in warm water.

2 Predict what will happen first. Then draw and write what happens.

⚠ Ask an adult to help with the warm water.

The first one has been done for you.

Solid	Will it dissolve?	Draw and write what happens
SALT	yes	The salt dissolved.
SUGAR		
SAND		

FLOUR		
SWEETS		

Think about it!

Did the sweet dissolve differently to the salt and sugar?

In what way?

_____

_____

CHECK YOUR LEARNING

◯ I know that some solids dissolve in water.

◯ I can look carefully to find things out.

4 Light and dark

The unit challenge

The activities in this Challenge unit will extend learners' knowledge of the following topics from the Learner's Book and Activity Book:

Topic	In this topic, learners will:
4.1 Light sources	recognise that there are many light sources and test their friends' knowledge
4.2 Darkness	understand that darkness is a lack of light and that without light we cannot see
4.3 Making shadows	know that shadows are caused when an object blocks light and use different materials to make darker and lighter shadows
4.4 Shadow shapes	see that shadows can have a shape that is different to the object that makes them and demonstrate this by making up their own story using finger puppets

Help your learner

In this unit, learners will collect evidence by making observations when trying to answer a science question and use first-hand experience (Sections 4.1–4.4). They will also make comparisons (Sections 4.1–4.3), ask questions, suggest ways to answer them and make suggestions for collecting evidence (Section 4.3). To help them:

1 Encourage learners to look at and use the key words in the glossary. They could make a wall poster as their own science glossary of light.

TEACHING TIP

Light is very familiar to us as we experience it every day. Make sure that learners are using scientific terms correctly. Sometimes learners will confuse 'shadow' and 'reflect'.

light, Sun, Moon, reflect

Is it a light source?

You will need a set of objects. Make sure some are light sources (for example a torch, a picture of a fire) and some are not (for example a mirror, a coin, a shiny object).

Remember:

A light source is something that makes **light**. The **Sun** is a light source.

1 **Test three friends. Do they know which are light sources? Can they say why? Fill in the table.**

Object	Friend's name	Is it a light source?	Why?
torch			

2 **Think about it!**

If you were on the **Moon**, would you see the Sun in the sky? _____

KEY FACT

In the night sky you can see small stars. Each tiny star is a light source.

The Moon is not a light source. The Moon **reflects** sunlight from the Sun.

CHECK YOUR LEARNING

◯ I know that light sources make light.

◯ I know that there are many light sources, including the Sun.

4.2 Darkness

What can your friends see in the dark?

You will need a box with a lid, black paper or fabric,
and dark, light and shiny objects.

1 Line the box with black paper or fabric.
Make a peep hole at the front.

2 Put each object in the box one at a time.
Test three friends. Which objects can they see?

Object	Name _____	Name _____	Name _____

3 Was one object easy to see? _____

Why? _____

4 Was one object hard to see? _____

Why? _____

Remember:

We cannot see if it is
completely **dark**. Our
eyes can only see if
there is some light.

CHECK YOUR LEARNING

◯ I know that darkness is when there
is no light.

◯ I know that we cannot see without
some light.

4.3 Making shadows

see-through, opaque, shadow

Dark and lighter shadows

You will need some **see-through** *and* **opaque** *materials, a torch, wooden or card sticks or tubes.*

Some objects make dark **shadows**. Others make lighter shadows.

1 Make some shadow puppets using different see-through and opaque materials.

2 Name some materials that make darker shadows.

_____

_____

3 Name some materials that make much lighter shadows.

_____

4 Design a test that will show you the best shadow-making materials. Say what you would do. Use your notebook to record this too.

I will test shadow-making materials by _____

_____

_____

_____

_____

Remember:

A shadow is made when an object blocks light. Shadows are dark because there is less light there.

KEY FACT

The Sun shines on the Moon and the Moon casts a shadow. Sometimes the Moon's shadow falls on the Earth. We call this an eclipse.

5 Think about it!

At night you sometimes have two shadows. Why?

_____

_____

CHECK YOUR LEARNING

○ I know that shadows happen when objects block the light.

○ I know that shadows are dark because there is less light there.

○ I know that different materials can make lighter or darker shadows.

Shadow finger puppets

You will need card, scissors, glue and a light source.

LOOK AND LEARN

The shape of your shadow can change depending on the position of the light source.

1 Make some shadow finger puppets and make up a story for the shadows.

2 In the story, move the puppets so that their shadows change shape or size.

3 **Think about it!**

When an aeroplane flies low, you might see its shadow race across the ground! What shape will the shadow be?

Remember:

You can change the shape of the puppet's shadow by sticking on a card hat or card hair. What other changes could you make?

CHECK YOUR LEARNING

○ I know that shadows can change their shape depending on the position of the light source.

5 Electricity

The activities in this Challenge unit will extend learners' knowledge of the following topics in the Learner's Book and Activity Book:

Topic	In this topic, learners will:
5.1 Electricity around us	identify items that use mains electricity and/or cells (batteries)
5.2 Staying safe	realise that mains electricity is very dangerous and conduct a survey to see what other people know
5.3 Making a circuit	recognise a working circuit and know that a bulb uses electricity to make light
5.4 Using motors and buzzers	carry out investigations with motors and buzzers
5.5 Switches	understand that electricity can be turned on and off using switches and build a two-way switch

Help your learner

In this unit, learners will talk about risks and ways to avoid danger (Section 5.2) and use a variety of ways to tell others what happened (Section 5.3). They will also use first-hand experience (Sections 5.1, 5.4 and 5.5), make predictions (Sections 5.4 and 5.5), identify simple patterns and recognise that a test or comparison may be unfair (Section 5.4). To help them:

1 Remember that electricity can be a difficult concept for learners because they cannot see it. Encourage them to make circuits and talk about what they see happening.

Learners should only ever handle low voltage cells and batteries (1.v – 9v). They should learn about the serious danger of mains electricity and to avoid contact with mains plugs, sockets and switches, and any damaged mains wires or components. They should also learn about the danger of liquids and electricity.

5.1 Electricity around us

Does it use cells or mains electricity?

Electricity is very useful. It makes lots of machines work.

Remember:

A cell is often called a **battery**.

1 Look at the pictures. Do they use **cells**, **mains electricity** or both? Fill in the table.

hair dryer   television   laptop   mobile phone   radio   torch

Machine	Uses cells only	Uses mains only	Uses cells and mains
hair dryer		yes	

2 Look around your home or school for more electrical machines. Write them here.

_____

_____

KEY FACT

We often throw away old cells and batteries. They are very bad for the environment. Always try to **recycle** them.

3 Think about it!

If you could invent a new electrical machine, what would it be?

_____

CHECK YOUR LEARNING

◯ I know that electricity is very useful.

◯ I know that electricity comes from the mains or from cells.

Safety poster

To stay safe	What is the danger?
Only put plugs into a mains socket.	Or you could get an electric shock.
Never put too many plugs in a mains wall socket.	
Never let young children play with mains electricity.	
Never leave cables across the floor.	
Never touch a switch with wet hands.	

Finish the poster. Choose sentences from below.

You could get an **electric shock**.

People could trip.

They could get an electric shock.

It could start a fire.

Safety survey

Carry out a **survey** to find out what three people know about the dangers of electricity.

1 First decide the way you will record the results.

_____

2 Use the words from the safety poster to ask three people if they know what to do to stay safe.

3 Record their answers here.

[blank box]

4 How many people knew all of the dangers? _____

5 How many knew about the danger of wet hands on switches?

_____

6 How many knew about the danger of fire? _____

CHECK YOUR LEARNING

◯ I realise that mains electricity is very dangerous.

◯ I know ways to keep safe around mains wires and sockets.

5.3 Making a circuit

circuit, bulb, working circuit

Playground circuits

You will need chalk, a playground and three friends.

These children have drawn a circuit on the playground. They are pretending to be electricity.

1 **Look at the speech bubbles. Fill in the gaps. Use these words to help you.**

cell   bulb   circuit

5 Electricity   **33**

2 Now draw the circuit on the playground and play the game with your friends. Pretend to be electricity and tell the story of your journey around the circuit.

Will these circuits work?

A   B   C

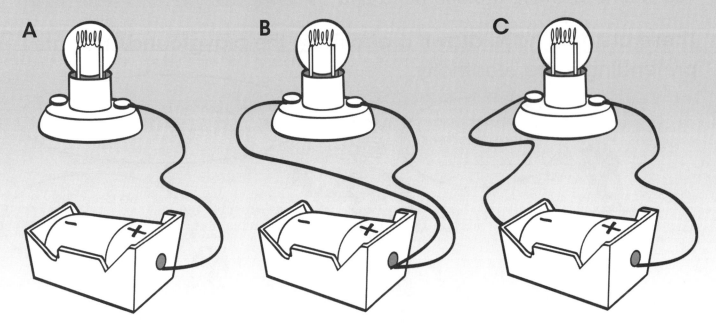

Look at the circuits above. Fill in the table.

Circuits that would work	Circuits that would not work

CHECK YOUR LEARNING

◯ I can recognise a **working circuit**.

◯ I know that a bulb uses electricity to make light.

5.4 Using motors and buzzers

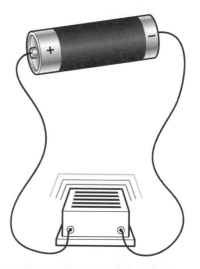

wire, buzzer, motor

More cells, more noise?

You will need **wire**, *cells and a* **buzzer**.

Remember:

A buzzer will only work if the red wire is connected to the positive (+) side of the cell or battery.

You are going to test whether adding more cells to a circuit will mean the buzzer makes more noise.

1 Plan your test here.

My question	If I add more cells, does the buzzer make more noise?
My prediction	
First I will	
Then I will	
What I found out	

2 Carry out your test. Was your prediction correct? _____

3 Did you notice a pattern? If so, what was it?

_____

4 Why did this happen? _____

5 Was this investigation a fair one? _____

What happens to the motor if I turn the cell around?

*You will need wire, a **motor**, a buzzer, a cell and sticky tack.*

1 Make a circuit like this. Put the sticky tack
on the motor so that you can see which
way the motor spins.

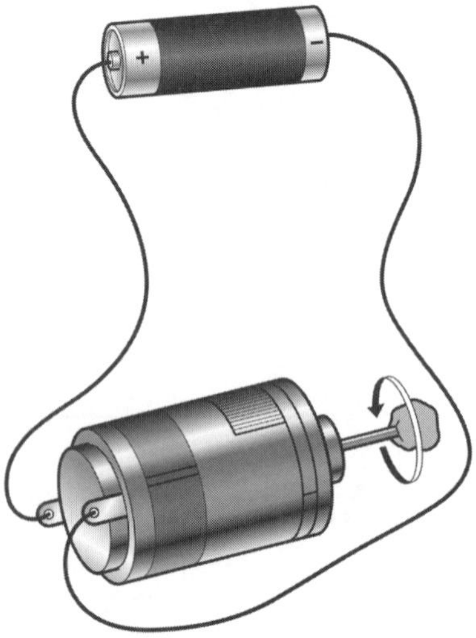

2 Predict what will happen if you turn the
cell around.

_____

3 Now try it out. What did you see?

_____

4 Try this several times to check that it always works.

5 Now try this test with the buzzer. First predict what will happen.

_____

6 Test the buzzer. What happened?

_____

7 Think about it!

Motors can change direction. In what way could this help a car that has electric motors?

_____

_____

CHECK YOUR LEARNING

◯ I know that motors use electricity to make things turn and buzzers use electricity to make a sound.

◯ I know that if you turn the cell, a buzzer will not work and a motor will work but change direction.

Make a switch from card

You will need card, wire, scissors, two paper fasteners, a steel paper clip, a cell, a bulb and a bulb holder.

Look at this circuit. It is not complete because the switch is not closed. The electricity cannot flow.

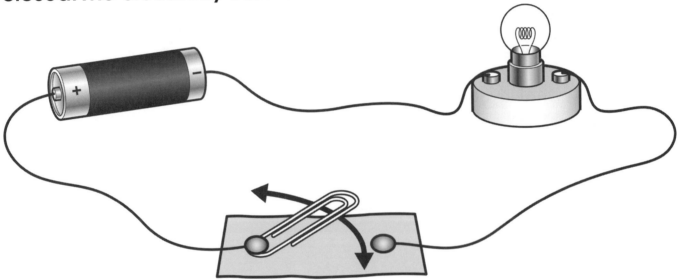

1 **What can you do to make the electricity flow?**

_____

2 **Make this circuit with the switch.**

3 **This switch uses a steel paper clip. Can you think of another object to use?**

_____

_____

> **KEY FACT**
>
> Switches are all around us. A computer has around 60 keys – each one is a switch.

Make a two-way switch

You will need wire, scissors, three paper fasteners, a steel paper clip, a cell, two bulbs and two bulb holders.

Look carefully at this switch.

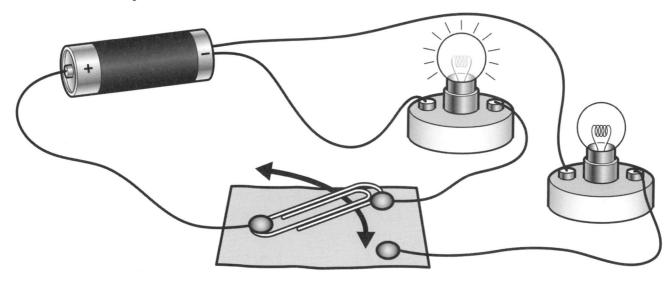

1 The paper clip can swivel to touch either of the paper fasteners. What will happen if the paper clip is moved?

_____

_____

2 Try making this circuit. Can you use the switch to control the lights?

_____

3 **Think about it!**

You have made a two-way switch. Traffic lights could use a three-way switch. Talk about the way this would work.

CHECK YOUR LEARNING

◯ I know I can change the flow of electricity using switches.

6 The Earth and the Sun

The unit challenge

The activities in this Challenge unit will extend learners' knowledge of the following topics from the Learner's Book and Activity Book:

Topic	In this topic, learners will:
6.1 Day and night	learn that we get day and night because the Earth spins
6.2 Does the Sun move?	see Skills Builder, Section 6.2
6.3 Changing shadows	observe that shadows move slowly as the Earth spins recognise that shadows are short when the Sun is high and long when the Sun is low

Help your learner

In this unit, learners will use first-hand experience (Sections 6.1 and 6.3), collect evidence by making observations when trying to answer a science question (Section 6.3), make predictions (Section 6.3), take simple measurements and identify patterns (Section 6.3). To help them:

1 Remember these abstract ideas can be hard for learners to visualise. Encourage them to model ideas (such as the spin of the Earth in Section 6.1).

TEACHING TIP

When learners model the Earth in Section 6.1, ensure that they spin slowly and anticlockwise so they can observe night, sunrise, day and sunset.

day, night, spin, midday, sunset, sunrise

Spin to see day and night

You will need a torch and a friend to work with.

The children are modelling day and night.

The torch is the Sun. The girl's head is planet Earth.

I cannot see the Sun. For my face, it is night.

If she only looks forward and slowly spins on the spot she will see the Sun rise until she faces it full on.

It is **midday**. The Sun is overhead.

If she continues to turn slowly, she will see sunset and then night time.

1 Try this out for yourself. Spin slowly but take care not to turn your head.

! Be careful not to look directly at the light from the torch.

2 Do you see **sunrise** and sunset?

_____

3 Keep turning slowly. Do you go through day, night and back to day again? _____

4 Swap places with your friend. Do they see sunrise and sunset?

_____

5 Talk with your friend about what they see. Is this a good model of the Sun and the Earth?

_____

_____

KEY FACT

The Earth spins once every 24 hours so we get about half as daytime.

6 **Think about it!**

If the Earth spun in just ten hours, what would happen to the length of our daytime?

_____

CHECK YOUR LEARNING

◯ I know that we get day and night because the Earth spins.

6.3 Changing shadows

sundial, unfair

Make a sundial

You will need card, sticky tack, a straw and chalk.

Sami has made a **sundial.** If he puts it in the same place each day, he can tell the time. If he moves it each time, the test will be **unfair.**

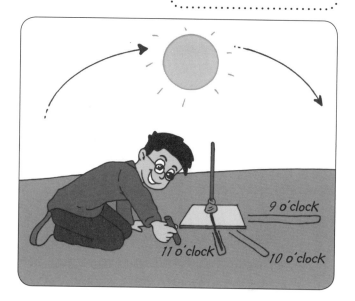

1 Sami has drawn the shadows at 9 o'clock, 10 o'clock and 11 o'clock. Can you see the pattern?

2 Now make your own sundial. Put it in sunlight and mark the shadows at different times. Measure the length of the shadows.

Time	Shadow length
_____ o'clock	_____ cm
_____ o' clock	_____ cm
_____ o'clock	_____ cm

3 **Think about it!**
Your shadow could be longer than the shadow of a tall tower! True or false? _____

CHECK YOUR LEARNING

◯ I know shadows move slowly as the Earth spins.

◯ I know shadows are short when the Sun is high and long when the Sun is low.

Answers

1 Going outside

1.1

Comparing environments

Answers will depend on the environments chosen and the animals found.

1.2

Looking after forests

1 gone down ☑

2 There might be fewer birds because there are fewer trees for them to nest in or because there is less food for them to eat.

3 Think about it!

We can protect animals by planting new trees when we cut others down or by using recycled paper.

1.4

Extreme weather

1 20 °C, 26 °C, 40 °C

2 Wednesday

3 35 cl, 9 cl, 0 cl

4 Monday

5 Think about it!

2 Looking at rocks

2.2

Which rock makes a good roof?

1 Chalk

2 Sandstone

3 Slate

4 Slate

5 Think about it!

The number of drops of water on each rock.

2.3

Water in soil

1 Use the same amount of water for each soil. ☑

Measure the water after two minutes both times. ☑

2 and **3** Answers will depend on the soils used.

4 The soil that let the least water though can hold more water for the plants. (The plants need the water in the soil, not the water in the measuring jug!)

5 Think about it!

Water is a natural material that comes from rain.

3 Changing materials

3.1

Changing materials

2

Object	Material	Bend	Squash	Stretch	Twist	Is it rigid or flexible?	Is it elastic?
sheet of paper	paper	✓	✓	✗	✓	flexible	no
paper clip	metal	✓	✗	✗	✓	flexible	no
rubber band	rubber	✓	✓	✓	✓	flexible	yes
coin	metal	✗	✗	✗	✗	rigid	no
ruler	plastic	✓	✗	✗	✓	flexible	yes

3 Think about it!

The paper clip is flexible because the metal is thin. The coin is rigid because the metal is thick.

3.5

Dissolving different solids

2

Solid	Will it dissolve?	Draw and write what happens
SALT	yes	The salt dissolved.
SUGAR	Depends on learner's prediction.	The sugar dissolved.
SAND	Depends on learner's prediction.	The sand did not dissolve.
FLOUR	Depends on learner's prediction.	The flour did not dissolve.
SWEETS	Depends on learner's prediction.	The sweet dissolved slowly.

3 **Think about it!**

It dissolved very slowly. (It may have coloured the water.)

4 Light and dark

4.1

Is it a light source?

1 This table should be completed. For example:

Object	Person's name	Is it a light source?	Why?
torch	Kim	yes	It makes light.
	Chan	no	It reflects light.
	Do	yes	It's electric.

2 **Think about it!**

Yes, if you were on the Moon, there would be times when you would see the Sun. During night on the Moon you would not see the Sun.

4.2

What can your friends see in the dark?

2 The learner will have completed the table.

3 The learner will identify whether any objects were easy to see and explain why, for example the object was a light colour.

4 They will say if one object was particularly hard to see and explain why, for example the object was black.

4.3

Dark and lighter shadows

1 The learner should make two sets, one of materials that make darker shadows and one of materials that make lighter shadows.

2 The learner should suggest more opaque materials, such as wood, thick fabric, card, foil, and so on.

3 The learner should suggest more see-through materials, such as thin paper, thin fabric and so on.

4 They should set out a test that would allow them to show that some materials make a darker shadow and others make a lighter shadow. They should mention a light source such as a torch and different materials they might test. They should explain that they observe darker and lighter shadows. They might say that they will record the observations, for example in notes, on a chart or with a camera.

5 **Think about it!**

At night there might be more than one light source (such as the two streetlights in the picture).

4.4

Shadow finger puppets

1 and **2** The learner will make some shadow finger puppets and make up a story about them. The story will include shadows changing shape or size.

3 𝕋𝕙𝕚𝕟𝕜 𝕒𝕓𝕠𝕦𝕥 𝕚𝕥!

When a plane flies, it casts a shadow that is often shaped like a plane. However, if the plane is flying on its side the shadow may be a long oval.

5 Electricity all around us

5.1

Does it use cells or mains elecricity?

1 The following table should be completed:

Machine	Uses cells only	Uses mains only	Uses cells and mains
hair dryer		yes	
television		yes	
laptop			yes
mobile phone			yes
radio			yes
torch	yes		

2 Other electrical items might be a ceiling fan, air conditioning, desktop computer, tablet computer, camera and so on.

3 𝕋𝕙𝕚𝕟𝕜 𝕒𝕓𝕠𝕦𝕥 𝕚𝕥!

Any sensible suggestion for a new electrical device is acceptable.

5.2

Safety poster

To stay safe	What is the danger?
Only put plugs into a mains socket.	Or you could get an electric shock.
Never put too many plugs in a mains wall socket.	It could start a fire.
Never let young children play with mains electricity.	They could get an electric shock.
Never leave cables across the floor.	People could trip.
Never touch a switch with wet hands.	You could get an electric shock.

Safety survey

1 to **3** The learner should have planned their survey, carried it out and recorded the results.

4 to **6** The learner should have answered the questions correctly based on their data.

5.3

Playground circuits

1 The speech bubbles should be completed as follows:

I am electricity moving to the bulb.

I am being pushed by the cell/battery around the circuit.

I have been pushed around the circuit by the cell/battery.

2 The learner draws a circuit on the playground and plays with other children as if they were electricity flowing in one direction around the circuit. They talk about their journey around the circuit.

Will these circuits work?

1

Circuits that would work	Circuits that would not work
C	A, B

5.4

More cells, more noise?

1 The table should be completed in a sensible way but does not have to be perfect. For example:

My question	If I add more cells does the buzzer make more noise?
My prediction	If I add more cells the buzzer will get louder.
First I will	Test the buzzer with one cell and listen to the noise.
Then I will	Test the buzzer with two cells and listen to see if it louder or quieter.
What I found out	I found that when I added a cell to the circuit the buzzer got louder.

2 yes or no

3 The learner should refer to a pattern of increased noise. That is, as cells are added to the circuit the buzzer will get louder.

4 An explanation might be – there was more electricity or more push or more energy.

5 yes or no

What happens to the motor if I turn the cell around?

2 Any sensible prediction, for example the motor will turn to the left.

3 Any sensible observation is reported, for example it turned to the right.

5 Any sensible prediction, for example it will work.

6 The buzzer will not work.

7 **Think about it!**
This could help a car go forwards and backwards. (It could also help with turning.)

5.5

Making a switch from card

1 The paper fastener should be swivelled so that it touches the other paper fastener.

3 The learner might suggest another metal object.

Make a two-way switch

1 The learner should be able to talk about the way the switch works.

2 The learner should report if they were able to make a working circuit.

3 **Think about it!**
The learner may be able to talk about the way a switch could control the flow of electricity to three different bulbs.

6 The Earth and the Sun

6.1

Spin to see day and night

1 to **4** The learner should talk about the way they and their friend see sunrise, sunset, day and night.

5 The learner should talk about whether this model helps them to understand the concept of day and night.

6 **Think about it!**
The day would be shorter – about five hours.

6.3

Make a sundial

1 The learner should refer to the shadow moving and getting shorter.

2 The table should be completed with suitable times and shadows that get longer or shorter.

3 **Think about it!**
True, the learner's shadow could be taller than the tall tower. When the Sun is low, the learner's shadow could be 5 m long. With the Sun very high, a tall tower may have a shadow just 1 m long!

Glossary

different	not the same
environment	a place where animals and plants live
extreme	very great or severe — for example extreme cold means very, very cold
forest	a place where lots of trees grow
measure	to find the size or amount of something, for example length or time
paper	a thin flexible material we use for writing and drawing on
predict	to say what you think will happen
protect	to look after something
rain gauge	something used to measure how much rain falls
temperature	how hot or cold something is
thermometer	something used to measure temperature

Remember:

Practise saying these words aloud. Try to use them when talking about the topic.

2 Looking at rocks

chalk	a soft white rock that can be used for writing
fair (test)	a test where you only change one thing and keep the other things the same
sandstone	a rock made of sand with a rough sandy surface
slate	a grey, flat, waterproof rock
soil	the natural material on the surface of the Earth in which plants grow
waterproof	something that is waterproof does not soak up water

3 Changing materials

bend	to change the shape of an object so that it becomes curved or folded
dissolve	when a solid becomes part of a liquid, for example salt dissolves in water
elastic	an elastic material can stretch but then goes back to the shape it started as
flexible	able to be bent, twisted, stretched or squashed

rigid	a rigid material cannot be bent, twisted, stretched or squashed
squash	change the shape of an object by pushing or crushing it – making it shorter 
stretch	change the shape of an object by pulling – making it longer or wider
twist	change the shape of an object by holding one end and turning the other

4 Light and dark

dark	when there is very little light or no light
light	bright glow from a light source that allows us to see things
Moon	the large object that goes round the Earth and we see in the sky at night
opaque	not see-through
reflect	if something reflects light, the light shines back from that object
see-through	clear or very thin so you can see through it
shadow	an area of darkness we see when an object blocks light
Sun	the nearest star to Earth – it gives us light and heat

battery	a store of electricity, also called a cell
bulb	a glass ball or tube that lights up when electricity passes through it
buzzer	an object that makes a sound when electricity passes through it
cell	a store of electricity, also called a battery
circuit	a complete path that electricity can flow around
connected	joined together
electric shock	when electricity goes into your body – a big shock can hurt or kill you
electricity	we use it to make things like lights, computers and televisions work
mains electricity	powerful electricity we use in buildings
motor	an object that uses electricity to make something move
recycle	use a material again
steel	a strong, bright, shiny metal
survey	information we collect by asking other people questions
switch	something that can break the flow of electricity in a circuit
wire	a piece of metal that electricity flows through – we use it to connect things in a circuit
working circuit	a loop that electricity can flow around

Remember:

Practise saying these words aloud. Try to use them when talking about the topic.

day	the time when a place on Earth is facing the Sun – the hours of daylight
midday	the time when the Sun is highest in the sky
night	the time when a place on Earth is facing away from the Sun – the hours of darkness
spin	to turn round and round about a point
sundial	something that people can use to tell the time
sunrise	the time when a place on the Earth turns to face the Sun
sunset	the time when a place on the Earth turns away from the Sun
unfair (test)	a test where you change more than one thing